This book belongs to

....

(witch in training)

Spells
for
self~improvement

Lauren White

**Andrews McMeel
Publishing**

Kansas City

✮ CONTENTS ✮

ancient book of spells

chapter

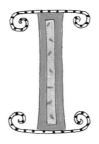

How to use this book

Magic has been used for thousands of years to make life generally a bit more fun! So if you want the key to success the easy way read on.

☆ THE SPELLS ☆

A brief description at the start of each spell
will tell you, at a glance, its uses and
applications.

There is also a key that gives a guide
to the difficulty, reliability, and timing of
each spell.

DIFFICULTY	TIME TAKEN	RELIABILITY
✳ ✳ ✳	⭐	⭐ ⭐

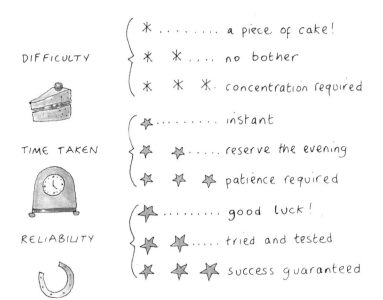

DIFFICULTY

* .... a piece of cake!

* * .... no bother

* * *. concentration required

TIME TAKEN

★ .... instant

★ ★ .... reserve the evening

★ ★ ★ patience required

RELIABILITY

★ .... good luck!

★ ★ ..... tried and tested

★ ★ ★ success guaranteed

As you become more expert you may want to adapt or personalize some spells~ or even devise your own. Remember YOU are in control of the power you give each spell. It's up to you.

Spell making is like cookery: Good ingredients and lots of practice produce the best results.

✰ Look up your chosen spell well in advance so that you can gather your ingredients.

✰ Take time to create the right atmosphere.

✰ You don't need solemn silence for most spells; it's often fun to perform magic in a group ~ just ensure everybody has plenty of time and space.

witches' hat

chapter

Spell casting ~ general hints and tips

· a big bag of magic things ·

your big bag of tricks should contain:

oils

pins

herbs

flowers

crystals

thread

candles

jars

You may wish to include eye of toad and tail of newt, but to be honest, it's not strictly essential!

✫ CHOOSING A WAND ✫

A wand is a very personal object.

The traditional wand

Traditionally,
a wand is cut from a birch tree with
a silver sickle under a new moon.

However, you can make or customize your own.

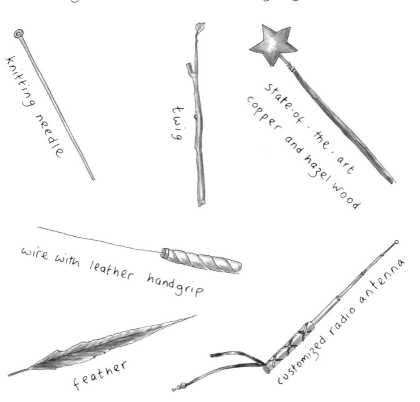

knitting needle

twig

state-of-the-art
copper and hazel wood

wire with leather handgrip

feather

customized radio antenna

too big

too curly

too untidy

perfect!

... can take a long time!

Red- energy, passion.

Green- understanding,
forgiveness, peace.

Yellow - hope,
activity.

In magic, different
colors represent
different moods
and energies.

Purple- wisdom,
solemnity.

White- purity.

Blue- stability, hope.

Pink- true love,
honesty.

Orange- action
warmth, cooperation.

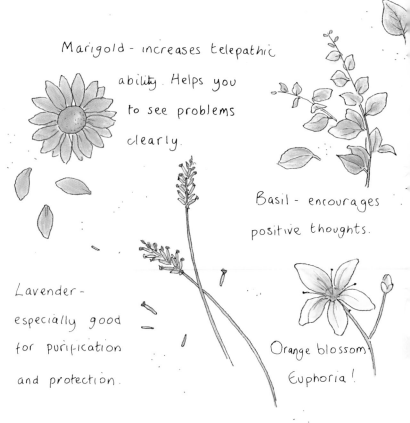

✿ THE MAGIC OF FLOWERS ✿

Marigold - increases telepathic ability. Helps you to see problems clearly.

Basil - encourages positive thoughts.

Lavender - especially good for purification and protection.

Orange blossom - Euphoria!

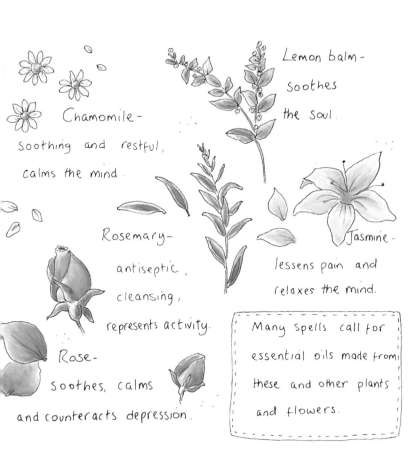

Chamomile -
soothing and restful,
calms the mind.

Lemon balm -
soothes
the soul.

Rosemary -
antiseptic,
cleansing,
represents activity.

Jasmine -
lessens pain and
relaxes the mind.

Rose -
soothes, calms
and counteracts depression.

Many spells call for
essential oils made from
these and other plants
and flowers.

Just a couple of extra points...

Witchcraft is just that — a CRAFT, a bit like wood carving or knitting. It takes time and patience to perfect!

Remember - Always buy organic (if you can).

A NOTE OF CAUTION

Please remember to dispose of potions CAREFULLY.

Some scientific studies have shown that too much undiluted magic can find its way into the water supply and wreak havoc!

"eye of toad!"

c h a p t e r

Winning friends and influencing people

HOW TO SHINE

This spell is particularly useful for parties, interviews, etc. – anytime you want to "shine."

DIFFICULTY	TIME TAKEN	RELIABILITY
*	★	☆ ☆

QUICK, EASY, AND SURPRISINGLY EFFECTIVE!!!

YOU WILL NEED

bell

Small star
(cut out from card?)

Marjoram
(Quiets the mind, calms the soul)

METHOD

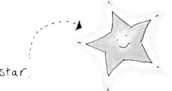

(i) Visualize yourself as the star.

(ii) Place your star on a flat surface and sprinkle with the marjoram.

. . . .tinkle . . . . .tinkle . . . .tinkle . . . .

(iii) Ring the bell and everyone around will be drawn to the shiny new you!

(iv) Carry your star with you for extra confidence!

JELLY BEANS CALLING

This is a spell designed to summon a special person. You don't have to use jelly beans but you can eat what's left over if you do!

DIFFICULTY	TIME TAKEN	RELIABILITY
* *	*	* *

NOTE

This spell is for encouraging a friend or loved one to contact

you. Use it sparingly as it's not fair to
have everyone at your beck and call.

☆ YOU WILL NEED ☆

colored thread

photograph

jelly bean (button,
colored counter, gum drop, etc.)

It is the power of color that connects with your chosen subject's spirit, so it's vital to get this bit right.

✬ M E T H O D ✬

(i) Choose a color that represents your subject:

i.e. "Jane" is bold and loud =

So choose a RED jelly bean and thread.

(ii) Tie the thread around "Jane's" photograph

and leave it for at least one hour to absorb
her energy.

(iii) Using the thread, tie the jelly bean
    around your telephone.

(iv) Eat the remaining jelly beans while
    you wait for the telephone to ring.

THE SECRET OF MAGNETISM

This spell works very successfully for increasing sexual attraction, so use with great care!

DIFFICULTY	TIME TAKEN	RELIABILITY
✳ ✳	★	☆ ☆ ☆

☆ YOU WILL NEED ☆

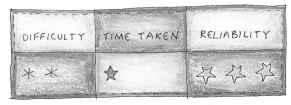

RED

★ 1 small piece of ferrous metal

★ (Iron, steel etc ~ Non-aluminium tin cans will do)

Daylight -

warm windy weather

It is useful to have a washing line but almost anything will do!

The aim of the spell is to transfer the "attractive" properties to the apple which when consumed will imbue you with the same properties. Sadly, the effects are quite short-lived...

METHOD

Simply hang up the   a) magnet

b) apple

c) metal

in that order, and leave for exactly one hour.

(Mind you don't get your strings tangled up!)

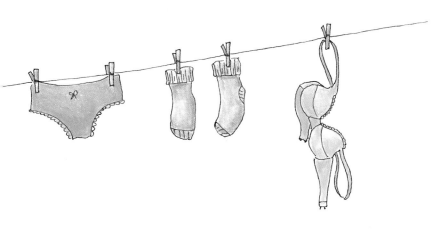

All you have to do next is eat the apple and you will find that people are drawn to you.

IT'S ~~MY~~ YOUR PARTY

If life seems a bit dull, a few interesting
invitations could liven things up. This is the spell
to summon them.   Simple!

DIFFICULTY	TIME TAKEN	RELIABILITY
✳	★ ★ ★	★ ★

✩YOU WILL NEED✩ an envelope   BLUE

a shell   sealing wax

pen + paper   ★ a toad   )

METHOD

come to me

(i) Light the candle.

(ii) Clear your mind and slowly write the words "come to me" ~ three times.

(iii) Seal this, with the shell, in the envelope.

(iv) Tuck under your pillow and sleep on it for one week.

(v) Get out your party dress!

Research into ancient and secret manuscripts has revealed that the performer of this spell would often keep a toad in a golden casket by the window to watch for visitors and messengers.

In the interests of animal welfare and convenience, it is not strictly necessary though.

Potion-measuring jug

c h a p t e r

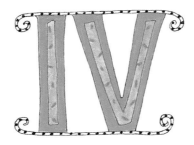

IV

Success... (the secrets of)

THE LIFE BUOY SPELL

DIFFICULTY	TIME TAKEN	RELIABILITY
✳ ✳ ✳	★	☆ ☆ ☆

This spell is for ensuring that any event goes smoothly. Your chances of a successful outcome at a party, job interview, or even a visit to the dentist will be greatly enhanced.

DRAWBACK

Could mean nocturnal activities!

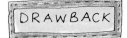

balaclava

flashlight

YOU WILL NEED

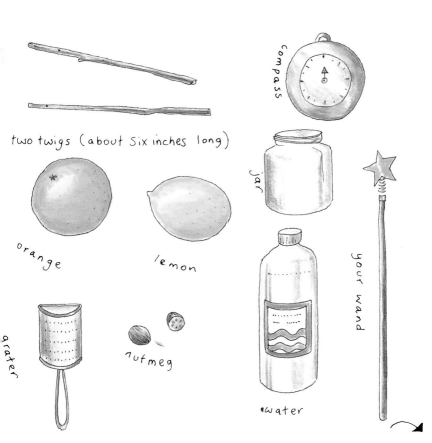

two twigs (about six inches long)

compass

orange

lemon

jar

grater

nutmeg

water

your wand

✬ METHOD ✬

(i) Cross the twigs so that they represent the
   points of the compass.

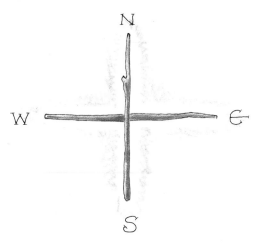

(ii) Grate the zest of the orange and the lemon and
   half of the nutmeg.

(iii) Place in the jar and add water.

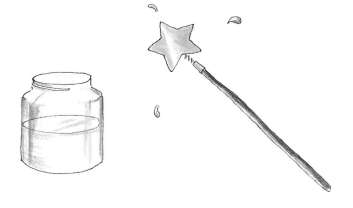

(iv) Take your wand and, with the tip, "flick" the water first to the north, then east, south, and west as dictated by the twigs.

This will ensure smooth sailing.

THE ART OF CONVERSATION

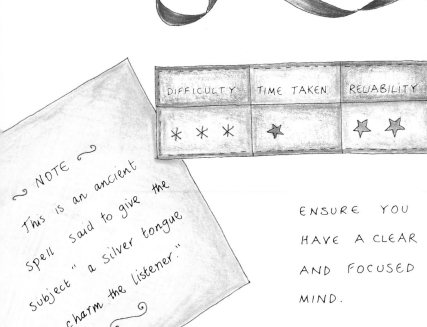

DIFFICULTY	TIME TAKEN	RELIABILITY
✳ ✳ ✳	⭐	⭐ ⭐

~ NOTE ~

This is an ancient spell said to give the subject " a silver tongue to charm the listener."

ENSURE YOU HAVE A CLEAR AND FOCUSED MIND.

This is an interesting spell that improves with practice. In this spell you must visualize the charm as your spirit and when it is tied up with the ribbon, it represents your flow of thoughts being "bound up." Therefore the moment you unwrap the charm ~ HEY PRESTO!!

☆ INGREDIENTS ☆

WHITE

small charm

(a spoonful)

PURPLE

(★ purple represents the mind)

METHOD

(i) Light the candle.

(ii) Tie the ribbon around the charm and leave it overnight.

(iii) Eat the spoonful of honey while you solemnly untie the charm.

(iv) Blow out the candle and enthrall everyone with your sparkling conversation!

RAGS TO RICHES IN ONE QUICK SPELL!

or

A simple cure for financial embarrassment

DIFFICULTY	TIME TAKEN	RELIABILITY
✱	✰ ✰ ✰	✰ ✰ ✰

This is a spell for conjuring up some much needed cash if the going is tough. It works by enabling you to see the opportunities that you may normally pass by.

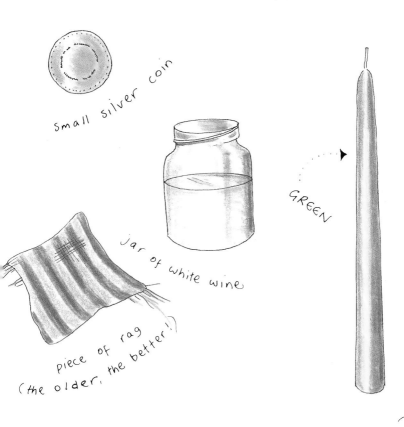

YOU WILL NEED

Small silver coin

Jar of white wine

Piece of rag
(the older, the better!)

GREEN

Green is a very auspicious color that attracts wealth. So, wear green when performing this spell.

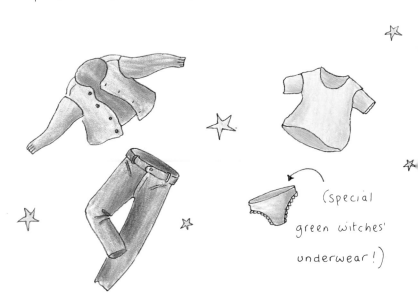

(special green witches' underwear!)

ON DAY ONE

(i) Light the candle (visualizing great mountains of gold coins helps).

(ii) Drop the coin into the wine and leave overnight.

(iii) Snuff out the candle.

(iv) Remove the coin in the morning and leave on a, window sill.

* * *

Repeat the procedure for five days.

* * *

ON DAY SIX, wrap the coin carefully in the fabric and bury in a secret place.

Sit back and let the cash roll in !!!

THE MIDAS TOUCH

This is an ancient spell for luck. It isn't about turning everything into gold, but it is about turning life into a golden opportunity!

DIFFICULTY	TIME TAKEN	RELIABILITY
✳	★	★ ★

NOTE

This spell must be performed in bright sunlight for best results!

YOU WILL NEED

three small yellow flowers
(buttercups are ideal)

pinch of turmeric

YELLOW

ear of ripe corn
(or teaspoon of
wholemeal flour in a pinch)

wristwatch

small quartz crystal

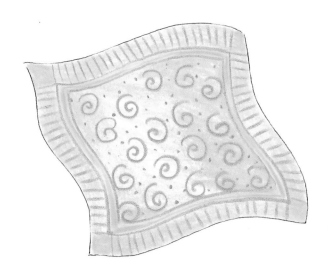

a large square of yellow fabric

If it is beautifully decorated and made of silk , all the better!

METHOD

(i) Lay out the silk square then wait for precisely five minutes.

(ii) Carefully place all of the ingredients on the fabric square...

wait five more minutes.

(iii) Tie up the bundle and hang it by an open window.

Golden opportunities will flood in.

THE RING OF CONFIDENCE

A quickie spell packed with elemental power!

DIFFICULTY	TIME TAKEN	RELIABILITY
✶	✶ ✶	✶ ✶ ✶

CAUTION

Do not wear stripes when performing this spell as they can interfere with energy transfer!

gold ring

(represents FIRE)

rose petals

(represent EARTH)

Salt

(represents the SEA)

BLUE

(represents AIR)

.PLUS.

some good white wine

This spell should be performed when the moon is waxing.
A thunderstorm provides the perfect conditions!

This spell will endow you with the :
PASSION of FIRE ∽ the STRENGTH of EARTH∽
the LIGHTNESS of AIR ∽ and the POWER
the SEA.

METHOD

(i) Light the candle.

(ii) Mix together the rose petals and a
handful of salt and "bury" the gold
ring in the mixture.

(iii) Sprinkle lightly with the wine.

(iv) Leave overnight.

(v) Slip the ring onto your finger and enjoy
your newfound elemental energy!

SHOWER POWER!

This is a spell to promote your own sense of motivation and empowerment! (WOW!!)

DIFFICULTY	TIME TAKEN	RELIABILITY
* * *	★ ★	★ ★

YOU WILL NEED

three small pebbles

one cupful of salt

a small handful of sand

NOTE This spell requires special conditions and some advance preparation but it is well worth waiting for the perfect moment.

* * *

in advance

* * *

Assess the weather and just BEFORE heavy rain or showers are due, do the following:

(i) Thoroughly mix together the sand and salt.

then, go outside and...

(ii) Lay the pebbles out :

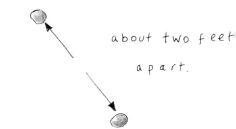

about two feet

apart.

(iii) Sprinkle the salt and sand between the
pebbles ⁓ to form a triangle.

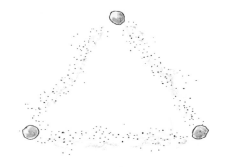

(iv) As the rain begins to fall, step into the center of the triangle and watch as the boundaries get gradually washed away.

(v) When just the pebbles are left, gather them up and save them.

This spell is enormously liberating ~ there will be no limits to what you can do!

wing of bat

chapter

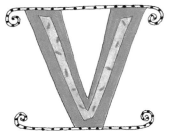

Beauty or the beast?

HAIR TODAY

A spell for beautiful tresses

DIFFICULTY	TIME TAKEN	RELIABILITY
* *	⭐	⭐

If you've ever wondered where the folklore about the benefits of washing your hair with fresh rainwater originated, it is probably based on this spell. Down through the ages many a glossy-maned witch has used it regularly.

☆ YOU WILL NEED ☆

Along with your bucket of fresh rainwater,

sock of a bald-headed man (poo!)

laurel leaf

★ ★ two currants

ivy leaf

(★) This is based on "reverse-logic" witchcraft:
a man with no hair will find all of his vigor
and energy in his feet (which may well be hairy!)

(★ ★) The original manuscript called for "eye of
newt" but currants will suffice!!

METHOD

Put ½ cup of rainwater in a bowl and add the laurel and ivy leaves plus the currants.

Carefully strain the liquid through the sock.

Finally...

gently "flick" the residual liquid over your head using the tip of your wand (if you have one), or use your index finger.

" Voilà ~ glorious hair !! "

WARNING   Do not immerse your hair in the mixture as it can promote very rapid and vigorous growth!

THE SLIMLINE SPELL

a

Quickie spell for the figure-conscious witch!

DIFFICULTY	TIME TAKEN	RELIABILITY
✶	⭐	⭐ ⭐

✦ YOU WILL NEED ✦

A tall, thin blue candle

A piece of spaghetti

one cinnamon stick

one matchstick (spent)

You may notice that all the ingredients have something in common: they're THIN.

one bay leaf

A long piece of string

METHOD

(i) Light the candle.

(ii) Bind all of the ingredients together (very tightly) with the string.

(iii) Place the bundle in a warm bath.

Performing this spell regularly will allow the water to "conduct" their characteristics. A new sylphlike you will emerge.

THE SECRET OF ETERNAL YOUTH

There are witches around today who are alleged to be several hundred years old. While this is difficult to prove, many are said to swear by this spell...

DIFFICULTY	TIME TAKEN	RELIABILITY
**	★★★	★

YOU WILL NEED

a new green leaf

a strip of orange peel

the tail of a mouse (!) ~ or

a piece of licorice

springwater

a dried prune

saucer

METHOD

(i) Place the prune in a bowl of spring water and leave overnight. Its "wrinkles" will have vanished.

(ii) Remove the seed from the prune and place this along with the other ingredients on a plain saucer.

(iii) Place the saucer beneath your bed for one month. During this time the items will all wrinkle and dry up while you remain dewy-skinned and youthful.

This spell should ideally be performed around the time of your birthday each year.

special spell-casting apron

chapter

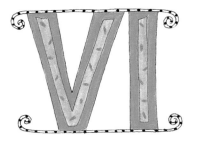

Having it all !

GETTING YOUR OWN WAY

NOTE OF CAUTION

Do please use this spell sparingly and with the best motives!

DIFFICULTY	TIME TAKEN	RELIABILITY
✳ ✳ ✳	★	★ ★

YOU WILL NEED

photograph of yourself

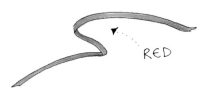

RED

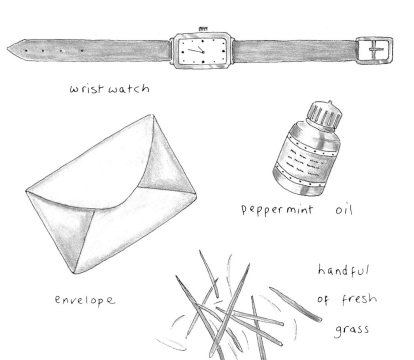

wrist watch

envelope

peppermint oil

handful
of fresh
grass

With judicious use of this spell, you will have
people falling at your feet.

METHOD

(i) Place the photograph and the watch in the envelope.

(ii) Tie the grass into a small bundle with the ribbon and sprinkle with the oil for added energy.

(iii) Place the bundle on top of the (sealed) envelope and leave overnight to absorb your energies.

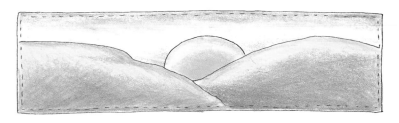

(iv) At sunrise, snip the ribbons and scatter
the grass to the four winds ⁓ this will
spread YOUR influence all around.

(v) Open the envelope, put on the wristwatch, and
jump three times. This will ensure that everyone
has time for you.

You have "center stage" for twenty-four hours
only - so make the most of it!

ADDED ZEST!

This is known as the "sparkle spell."

The idea is to "reuse" the energy of the new moon and have it in hand when you need some extra "Oomph."

DIFFICULTY	TIME TAKEN	RELIABILITY
⭐	⭐	⭐⭐⭐

CONDITIONS

Nighttime when
there is a new moon.

The success of this spell obviously depends
heavily on cloud conditions!

☆ Y O U   W I L L   N E E D ☆

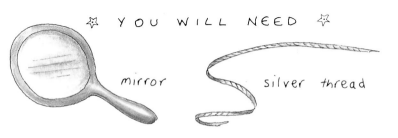

mirror   silver thread

·plus·

new green
leaf ~
(any sort)

small piece of purple
fabric (preferably silk)

NOTE

This spell can be
conducted either in the
open air or by a window. It is merely
essential that you are able to position
the mirror so that the moonlight is
shining directly onto it.

(i) Lay the mirror on a flat surface so that it can absorb the energy of the new moon.

(ii) Place the objects on it.

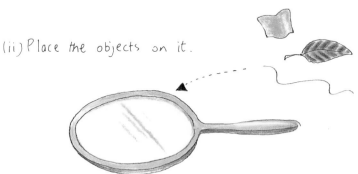

(iii) Simply wrap up the leaf in the fabric and tightly bind the little bundle with the silver thread.

NOTE

All you need to do is repeat the procedure to recharge.

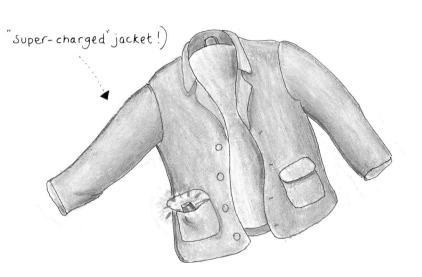

"Super-charged" jacket!)

When you need a boost simply place
the "energy bundle" in your pocket.
Carry it with you whenever you need a
bit of added "zest and sparkle!"

OPENING THE DOOR

Forget "feng shui" ~~~
this spell is all you'll ever need to
chase away bad vibes, energize
your space, and generally rev-up
the atmosphere.

DIFFICULTY	TIME TAKEN	RELIABILITY
* *	*	* * *

A NOTE ON MOONPHASE

This spell should be performed when there is a new moon – preferably in late winter / early spring.

YOU WILL NEED

a fine paintbrush

spring water

myrtle leaves

pine needles

your own door key

Wearing your favorite item of clothing will increase the potency of this spell.

METHOD

(i) Place the myrtle and pine needles in a bowl.

(ii) Add one cup of springwater.

(iii) Wait for the moon to rise to its highest point.

(iv) Place the key in the bowl.

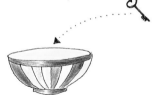

(v) With the paintbrush "paint" this water around
your doorway.

This will give it an immediate magical
energy.

(iv). The metaphorical door is now wide
open for good things to flow through.

OUT WITH THE OLD

A spell for a fresh start...

DIFFICULTY	TIME TAKEN	RELIABILITY
✶ ✶	✶	✶ ✶ ✶

Take a fresh green apple and remove the seeds.

You will also need :

    five drops of patchouli oil

    one clove of garlic

    one white candle

    A small piece of mirrored glass

    (foil will do if there's none on hand but

    glass works better)

. out with the old . . . in with the new .

METHOD

(i) light the candle and repeat the words:

OUT WITH THE OLD

IN WITH THE NEW

(ii) Place the garlic, oil, and the glass fragment in the center of the apple.

(iii) Place the two halves back together again.

(iv) Dig a small hole and bury the apple along with its new contents.

Meanwhile...

keep the pips in a small bag or box.

As the old apple returns to the earth, this little bag contains the seeds of your new beginning.

witches' shoe

c h a p t e r

VII

Emergency spells ~ for life's little problems!

BLOW AWAY THE BLUES

This spell is a quick blast of fresh air if you're feeling low.

☆ YOU WILL NEED ☆

photograph of yourself and a lock of your hair

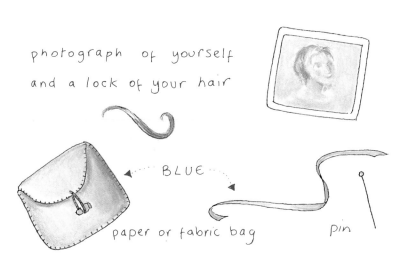

BLUE

paper or fabric bag

pin

☆ M E T H O D ☆

(i) Tightly bind the ribbon around your lock of hair.

(ii) Place this, the photograph, and the pin in your little blue bag.

(iii) Hang it from a tree or a high place.

With the first gust of wind your blue mood will be swept away on the breeze.

ON THE SPOT RELIEF

A simple 'witches' remedy for unsightly spots and blemishes, which we <u>all</u> know always pop up on the "big day."

☆ YOU WILL NEED ☆

A red wax crayon
The juice of three lemons
One large potato
A piece of cloth
Grater

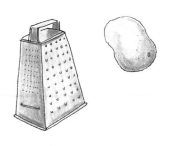

METHOD

(i) Using the crayon, draw "spots" on a
   window that is facing the moon.

(ii) Squeeze the lemons and grate the (peeled) potato
    into a bowl and mix well. Annoint the offending
    item on your face with the liquid.

(iii) Dip the cloth into the liquid and "erase" each
    spot from the glass (you could invent a song
    or chant for this).

(iv) As the spots disappear ～ so will yours!

WALK TALL

Placing an object in your shoe can have very powerful effects!

☆ **YOU WILL NEED** ☆

evergreen leaf
(see footnote)

salt

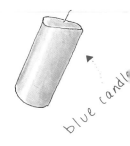

blue candle

METHOD

(i) Light the candle and sprinkle a ring of salt around it.

(ii) Briefly hold the leaf over the flame (don't singe your fingers!) and place it in your shoe ~ simple.

FOOTNOTE Evergreens provide a constant flow of energy that will give you a permanent spring in your step.

About the Author

"Adding a sprinkling of magic to the everyday" perfectly describes Lauren's original style of drawing. This is precisely what she does in her little books of spells.

Lauren lives in the Bedfordshire village of Cranfield where her family has lived for generations, although she studied fine art in Hull and London and worked as a wildlife illustrator before returning to the village. She shares what she describes as her "crumbling cottage" with her partner, Michael, and her "familiar," a little black dog called Jack. This is where she brews up her own spells and potions (of the gentlest kind), plays the piano, and stops the garden from invading the house!

Lauren loves drawing and always has a sketchbook in her pocket. In addition to her books of spells, Lauren has produced a series of six little gift books celebrating the simple things in life for MQ Publications, and her designs for Hotchpotch greeting cards are sold around the world.

First published by MQ Publications Limited
254-258 Goswell Road, London EC1V 7RL

Copyright © MQ Publications Limited 2000
Text and illustrations © Lauren White 2000

ISBN: 0-7407-0552-0

Library of Congress Catalog Card Number: 99-67079

1 3 5 7 9 0 8 6 4 2

Printed and bound in Italy